THE SAID
LANDS, ISLANDS, AND PREMISES

THE SAID

LANDS,

ISLANDS,

AND PREMISES

Mary Margaret Sloan

CHAX PRESS

Minneapolis 1995

ISBN 925904-13-9

Parts of this book appeared previously in *Acts, Big Allis, HOW(ever), Ironwood, Mirage, Raddle Moon, Re*Map,* and *Talisman.* Excerpts from *Infiltration* were published in a letterpress limited edition by Queriendo Press, Guadalajara.

Cover art: etching by Penelope Downs, *Infiltration,* Queriendo Press, 1989. Reproduced courtesy of the artist.

Published by Chax Press
Post Office Box 19178
Minneapolis, Minnesota 55419-0178
612-721-6063

Library of Congress Cataloging-in-Publication Data

Sloan, Mary Margaret
      The said lands, islands, and premises / Mary Margaret Sloan.
            p.   cm.
      ISBN 0-925904-13-9
      I.   Title.
PS3569.L548S25   1995
811'.54—dc20   95-21999
                                                                               CIP

for

George Sloan

and

Larry Casalino

with love

Table of Contents

Abeyance Series

would convene
a light a girder

voices apart leaving
will without conjugation

of objects deceiving
arrangement

let any number in warm nests
bring on weaving, retreating west or east
then go, stop, rest and start, without
in the least disturbing, reducing to both, to closed roads
an act continuing, comes
to believe, to tolerate a trail abandoned
burning of trees at the edge
as taught in the air of confusion, borrow or beg
two guesses, hands flailing
at the wheel, faces washed away
by air, by halves rushed through
locked up by day and by night to say
they are mouths isn't right
but ready to eat
part flower, fruit and feed
more than perfect divisions
a stain of green in the air
lastly the piece defective
if any animal equaled in glass
by clausal movements preserved
from their vegetation they arise
as wood or stone to depart, leaving their beds
by climbing, poised to shoot
exhibiting in such a light the rest
either heads or limbs, either arms or legs, any part
then go, stop, restart, mount
to dissolve a loose notion by merely filling
a treatment of the future or edge
leaving the bodies blank or untouched
to travel the shape as it comes apart

from the instrument
of great and permanent objects
shedding views

a perfectly flat field
of the target variety or self-reading
the hot hours stream east

an argument entirely absorbed
in catastrophe in a fault
is for can claim no similar advance

feeling to verify the constants
accumulating as a heat engine
now one now the other is ahead

timed as the sun
going out
to hold, and let go, and pull, and lift, and ward

just like them see them east to west to disposition
alert stone to noise to exile all direction

evidence withheld a river
running a reference system
falls bristled with the maker's mood
forerunner of the hysterical state
shift confusion
to a nearby speed

responsive to delay a new feature contriving
river as a series of rocks
surfaces ridged scarred burned
should have been a given
now white
ornate and abrupt changes
building fire precariously

what falls there are discarded
or wandering diagnosis on behalf
of filling the first white space on the map
rests in evening as advocates
recover the place jettison its beginning

sufficient spare
a summary influence
face to grass
confusion couldn't bear
could be heard without being seen

weather sectioned
timing scavenges
weak fixture whipping through
a lull in the wreck
gathers future numbers
bluish continuous object
the moods alone numbered
change sky beyond recognition
shakes to mute

print
catastrophe shelter
inexhaustible neglect
locked in

the incident in decline
independent of scale
summarize the landscape
cut from the sun
by default
maintaining eye contact
with the ground

piece together
curves imagined or known
out of hand under eyes
to a standstill

a body across its shape
as far as near as
local was as ever
a geological embrace recording
a ridge as night

inordinate perspective
a given overlooks
an allowance not to make
illusionary space
calling the sky
everything else

taken outside
the centerpiece of a moment
housing the tentative approach

to see what was being seen
given the magnitude of the tense
with amateur desperation
day half-conceived
in pacing
the entire procedure and medium of longing

be seen as little thing
less missing formation
to inhabit a feeling
disposed to take
the relative sense whereas

taken between slow winds
what's suppressed widens the breach
nature sleeps in
several sets confused
"to whom do you speak"
not asking
sleek or driven
needlessly to the interior
a sheltered air
gives up the function of keeping

drastic measures
an abeyance to precede or follow
last night
contains an extra day
stutter coincides
to kill burn and lock up
an ache between tides
broken gradually
to us

something locally authentic
details a former period
sacrificial injunction
in missing detail
ecstatic decorum embodied
exact correlation of one sorrow to one color
accepting on the face of it
gifts scaled to

the least decision elsewhere
part of a room comes to the door
a picture to life
stands impersonally for sorrow

a former countryside
with trees bushes hills rounded
by reasons outside the picture
repeats without a change
a wager to the mouth

this also to our minds
exploration reproduced
a background dwelling
on the water situation colors
playing at verges

leans out throwing shapes
appearances cultivate
diagonal chaos flinging
peroration to digression

when lighting is too many
a crew assigned to stars
barely can they plot
shapeless shapes
from now to on

predecessors left their things
asleep in active pastimes
shading most normal
things to do with a precipice

outside the viewer's reach
secure to walk on

stretched squares retreated
into birds sunk soaked stained
twisting a congress of willing circles

to petals equal to road
perforated in effect
by peering into

collisions divided
arms entwined
one lay
in the posture of the first fraction

replicate though petrified
shrouded in air
opening to be fed
locations coming going folding up

miniature canyon topography
blackened and hit
traveling a circumference of unknown miles
showers its character
weak but binding
applications revolve
crawl of thickness marauding
posture of the resultant
measure in hands and knees

touch exhausted regions substitute
mineral for irritant
arms pitted against torsos

all the time divides
sites flooding lines
to vantage point

outside the point addressed
crumbling until day
one still tilts by stars
just arrived kneeling
raining ground

bearing steady light
false clear rounding
the phase
walls failing edifice

what is choosing what
squirrels in the narrows
many times finds
more dark more wary

a convoy making
chance saves
a night chance
withdraws to itself
any century held over

foreign seas
to matter remaining quiet
within its folds
a likely choice
cosseted like ten nothings

limit the time or gauge
the white passage
where suspicion shores up the view
dredging a static celebration
a region of the water
in trouble sleeping
leaves a strange face behind
in the noise an air
of wild people
intractable selection evidence
so damaging to a false move
with nothing to it

discard minutes at the ruinous edge
a life sentence to the one
who bore last night's face
plain sight misleads
any speech showing favorites
coming back the same as
hungry and crazy
freeing water freezing

a gesture to drag
time hysteria's outlook
action pulls the actor in
to their eyes though unreadable
with indifferent agreement

same as the damaged one
or some other peril
commotion digests
the situation seeks nothing
give it a wide earth or a glass room
trusting accident

Rest

Of time relearning, formal progression constrains a wholeness of insight: weary of so long acting the simple past, empty country wanted to stand still and listen, no, one or less. Mountainous dark confines, indistinguishable sky, gathered to set in motion the tired walker. As many walking stream through hectic moral outlooks, behavior summarizes itself. Molten plant hurries to hands. Instead of being nocturnal in its habits, touring in obscure recesses, make use of this perversity, correct these steps

sleep seemingly caught something of the sky. (Caught in its image) (as) finding the partition of that artifact's dominions a plain ripple, a likelihood resistance wherein the confining mountains revealed a shape. Luminous, classless, climbing up the rough mass of central islands; scopic proliferation germinated future, imagined safety. Are not all so: if one just stamps the ground in slumber. A figure raises an arm to speak, goes awry. Climbing the rough mass, border conditions want more wants

mountainous shapes confine a town. A town may darken its limits; walls lead it, obscure in its recesses (folding) sleep (folding in) light of its own (in a fold in light of its own) peremptory animal theme self-possessed touring. What was a life thrown in relief against its species? Described contrition by outsider, from afar, a character, fabled metonymy. Maps of self-restraint. High metaphorical resolution of solicitude to others' thoughts. In any counterfactual heart of the world, multi-rational foraging sometimes excavate between devices change garden to wilderness, intercalated nocturne fugitive insert hilltops, mountain peaks, a surround, as nestling form; all calculations yield lowering, static, active, magnetic, inverting, reciprocal; device in blackness, light slope articulated soft cubes, town of sleeping heat, travail of limbs entwined, untended thoughts' phototropic rise in wind

passionless constructions no one cried out, dreamed in tandem. Forgiveness inventions seemingly misled, a form is given no nesting place. Erotic chronology, horizontal axis of rest in incalculable forgiveness. In didactic embrace a feeding culture document forecloses minor mania. Eyes are occupied, static romance. At the end of perception's grasp three dark sighs. Molten plant hurries to fingers. Discovery grazed, imagined creature(s) like a self, hungry animals looking in folds. This side of the body being tired, the other takes up the task

the figure seals itself in, one of us, momentary certitude as pronounced as hunger. Laboring surface, figure with two arms raised, empty body described in flame, distant ancestry races from a book at the periphery, figure on horseback riding a diagonal course rips a field of scattered trees, trees bare with two limbs upraised as arms, mutual greeting of rider and trees

"as for the likeness of living creatures" where mountains are flattened we have a field, one unlit figure; above are circling walkers in flight, birds with heavy wings, heavy with color, rustling, breeding light from noise, mercilessly forgiving: impulse gardens' disposable course

Like Trees, The Surface

succumb to the routine
of looking for a year

safeguarded against any terror
the sacrificial interrupted

how come we feel nothing
will fictionalize

or get to know
a study of demolitions

however wrong and hopeless as a guide
cling to summer

in spite of evidence of constant
velocity

if the plane takes a turn
involving sleep

in a great deal of trouble
to the hand divided

uneasy fixing ends as if
making nations out of land

could the surroundings
be free from our plan

till they came to rest
in perfect disorder

an obscure journey broken
where we found the wall
and its windows
invested with a depth
not traversable
thick where stone was soft
and gave in to our thoughts

whose upper hand
taking the corner slowly
the blue of the right angle bent
modified ease
the structure giving
something to crawl up or over
how it lived
scaling the vacuum
whether it was mouth
or hands or mind in use

it grew bringing more
intense ingredients to bear
on the realization lived in
thought to ways
of covering the wall
leaving it absent

it was or could be or has been
called white noise
or thought of as
the noise of nothing once
frightening and recurrent
borrowing when seen
this word or one word at least
that had been used

it had been the noise of a field
with two boundaries
perhaps in actuality the sound
of conjunction
or the sound of listening
to something simple
two boundaries with white field
seem like nothing
moves with all its elements
in place while
two entities of more
sophisticated but minute nature
made their exchanging journey

they had to go they went
across and crossing carefully
avoiding elaborate patterns
as if in the restricted
ample space avoidance
were an issue
only to find here
flat as paper
but still are madly careful
as regards word and station
warning where
nothing is immobile

deep windows
of flimsy solace
feel the walls moving in
removing day
different as
light relative to
building in air
where a room
is being
removed to stop
a flow

success did not come
the trees had no branches to see

an abyss of abysses, a riddle of riddles
to read the letter when it's a dwelling

an interior understood but nothing
is moved to find

the doors where help however
all fallacious

the character old and one's own
stationed between a place to go and a place

to live where uncanny currents
of labor leave as a trace

cries of workmen in palms and waves
grains below the surface moved
one realm of clouds
slid another more solid world
law or the like

reversing birds, speech and waves: occasions
of anything well in hand
will have to be imagined

even in our own sight, not magnified
tiny mountains and their land
a glaze of darkness with sky and water
more plentiful, similar

or missing, a wrong turn
could have been wanting
could be repeated slipping away
through the narrow mouth

where waves annul each other
defiant of observation
speaking heard in plain water
found wanting as music

to recover what had been said
mingled with mishaps a possible answer
the geometry of earth surrounded
and apparently surrounding

the divided sky
or the sky sorted itself
into artificial planes

to retrieve recognition from momentum
a question atrophied
as thought with abandon
person otherwise speechless

up early waiting for

the trees to explode
what had been dreamed

ahead of time was found
coming back as procession

where cloud moves or is
the rock echoing with false water

small false rock making
crazed lines careful

maps traverse the sun
arrows and rays inside

facing south the rock faces us
entering in reverse order

each blank tree with north facing ghost
an echo of the hoard of people foreseen

pace and expanse of speech
utter absence of traffic

aiding and abetting
its large clear windows
looked to where

the very fact of striking for solitude
the shiny artificial lake
with richly condensed horizon
into spaces however briefly
of dark blue upland
strong cloud shadow moved
in tortuous corridors

for mention may be made
of the achieved isolation
and many colored appeal
our portion surrounded and committed
other persons a numerous array
barely folded in
of the blessed diminishing
concentric zones

what should have looked on trees
looked on windows

where light assembled
according to persuasions

a day we all tried to find
what was exceptional

or available to a love of plants
building all its own

where on cloth with panes or frames
a portrait rested an animal

emerging from closed grounds
like trees the surface

framed difference in density
in one door another bloomed

shadows for giving vacancy
words for wind close up

sirocco mistral
austere messengers work below

unrecollected walls
roads, creations of any making
made hard and lateral
stone anything, paths
hindrances gather import
spurts of journeys permitted
with sluice-like action
of the love of not knowing
where that spot was what
hearing and sleeping with
thought a thing like
anything else

the one free lane
set aside assembly

barely there to get away
with water interests

without protection
a glass system lives

on into this century
that and four other rivers

with part missing or strewn
as we rise earlier

to discuss what room
fear or uncertainty takes up

alive in a world of waves
unless this view is loved

as what was made by accident
kept at one remove

to see smear
where first we tried our idea

The Argument Needs and Shall Receive

"come in under . . ."

Robert Duncan, "The Propositions"

that this circle be avoided because of
its violations landing dreams at usual
sets out in disarray inclined as the
wing toward immobility as the wing

      ripping
                retracts

to leave shadows a formal layout
tributaries cut for beginning or end to
"act as if you don't know where you
are" acquiesce

                  at once
   in the main

in a real way or as a hindrance elastic
intervals gave on to a quantity to be
covered in a given time on or beside
empty but for us sometimes together
sometimes as features of the interior
scatter

     makeshift
            wrenched
   inspired by

the resolving power feeling where it
came in elaborations to enhance a
memento as from each other as from
our suspension fictitious or

     unbridled
            beside itself

retrace the contents across the midst
seeing "what was that funny bird

sound" attenuated as well as
complicit in what lay outside to instill
in postures of animation

like touch
what comes after
out of reach

as a substitute serves fused with our
circular motion inquiring of
intermediaries divergence full of rips
arrays itself in flight
investigate
shock

springing responses to states of
vigilance this way and that was
natural unnatural or conferring
architecture on slight hesitations at
the periphery

be lenient

as ascending sharply invitation
streaks to the given well known to
inhabitants as "the reassuring
familiar look of things" undecided
inflection

undergoing
precision

half led leading unprepared to
causeways in unconfirmed breath
flight toward insight was a name or
handwriting inclusive

Infiltration

using the reciprocal   a tactical front
scrutiny starved   an early region drifting in
arrhythmia will   will not object
to the event   physically managed
bloodless consolation   housing an epoch
takes the place   whose
was whose   familiar area of skin
upholding   a discrepancy
or desertion   as were
proximate entreaties   dying down

either was   or was a set
for collision or engagement   abolished by section
a form of life relatively minor   shaded portions
weakening activity without   intimacy
briefly   savage like any

ordinary speaker
where might   motion in
a part of nature subsumed   crowding
assembled   shot through
with recollection   in the aftermath

to pass to another   through a lapse
as visible laments   reach the firing level
splice cutaneous heat   skimming
a population   with whom
no intercourse may be held

                                  as administration of
transitive arrests   must succeed
the whole sphere of   and yet no and yet
one looks   to stop
the other   is one of kindred
ferocity   anatomical substrates
of the refractory period   threw them
in a straight line   wouldn't
voluntarily submit   to being touched

to be moved into   put one's hand inside
between the date set and the time
                    deletes insidious guesses
holding them   to another sleep
a region crossed   with camouflage
        compelling an ecstatic course of errors
those issued in the brutal way
listing   spans the mechanism
powerless to deflect   sometimes long after
anywhere starts unless

inclinations	edge
without article	at rest or of uniform
mind	to mouthe
as they passed	into the capacity
containment	tears to pieces
try signals	to the takers
a city struck	breathing
sweet and unusual	recklessly

wondering holds them immediately after

transgression if it were

                        in a shadow depression

between words   the injury records

for words   restless associations

still in thrall   go if it were

taken down   falls away by degrees

steep in the cut   parallactic custody

wild   to be a part of things

circulating   in the living subject

gestures of   change that

to supply   every reason to believe

filling a depression created

                    by previous activity

fitted for burning   nervous pleasures
maneuver to these ends   the transitive setting
fascination wrapped   inside command color
and sloping   continues in its state
allowed to drag along the ground   even
moving ends in tuft-like branches   halfway
through the sentence   a sphere apart
by reason of endless weeping   engaged
an action carried   through omission

fictile details   halfway through
unrestricted fixed conditions   also inform
autonomous land   driving through passing
all space has withheld   when
causing those who sleep
                     entering somewhat recklessly
to speak   not to detect and avoid
this annexed affection   in territorial surges
                                  thousands transported

afferent incision
differ with the reasons
torn to pieces in the dark
attempting to evade
self sustaining
reconnaissance
acquisitive centers
falling through
a fit of stamina without

details
days etched in

impulses random
minor slip or failed
impressed upon
sites washing over
none still alive

charged wherever   encouraged
within some thousand years   trespassing
with little intermission   a topical siege
in the burnt district   capricious inability
campaigning   to work the lock
the passage   is the improbable event
urged to justify   delirious adaptation
strategic to   a very body
is its oblivion   with one word concealed
am all forgotten

go forth to specious holdover   landing sets
small currents   to plan
recovery from the pressure of a footstep
and direction   may be held
remotely to each   day's moods driving
inaccuracy   pitiless applications
secure iconic populace   fielding
processes embedded   as ambient equations
state of rest   to come
reoccupy attempts once destroyed

unloved   the witnesses whose traces
administer in silence   teaching precaution
need be dreamed as wasted   teaching them
to set fire   to its natural element
rigged by violence   compositions unearthed
magnetic summons   glancing off
facts or events   storage
grotesque but within normal range
                          seeming to want to be alive
to connect nothing   devising
alarmed   states
by force   with nothing undone
adhering to each   others' fortunes
                                 were consumed

face in the day of action   ingress
shiftlessly accumulating   an indefinite leave
almost touching   a law abiding air
set in motion   glassed in centuries
as passing into other rooms
embedded in their processes
flames rolled over them instantaneously
                                  obliged to arrest
a line unless   going close
their progress   set in stone
an extemporaneous slip   with no object
some are led   to distrust the transit making
correction   for earth's curvature
adjustments do   something microscopic

Patience, Antithesis

could speak better as a body
whose cadences came
soothing and lacking
an ethic of moods
from former decades

trees in their route
of invisible sets
could set a tone without guile
or moving where purpose
moves backwards as animals

turn thought after thought
into never-ending events
kept from distance
even in the ground
with sounds from time to time

all unwilling gestures
effusions of place
of gaze intact
insufferable thoughts

reverse our selves
say there we are
under rigid locution
but now there is time

at least to know
parts of us lost
diffused into what
was begun not with excuses

content to be local
while excesses languish
which could unfold
the disastrous tale

drawn by every stratagem
healthy vivid with never
a sign we are here
in annunciation so arresting

not a belief in preference
forgetting so many things

cues always changing
after time of decay

in chained surrounds blue
letters for glow, rip or rest

keeping in shape
a shrine to the covert

all that's different
altered in being said

an outcropping as an abandoned part
of lingering as words
to use and what not for what
is happening or would be

as present tensions make out
what's moody loving change
excluded remnant sections
of scale collapsing an immediate

relief in curvature's wandering plane
never as far as a refuge
soon to be lost or diminished
in what was taking place

couldn't be taken in with all
the self-canceling effects
as if by the outcast position
a brief territory absorbed

in boundaries taken on faith
in address not personal but the matter
as all effects out of place
nothing contained as supposed

to be a nexus in pieces
side to side disturbed
poised to tell what's surmised
from noise we made

transferred the day
but not its conditions
to the value of a hill as is
descent into circumstance

from inside and behind
a provision for surface
reactions thought
up from beneath

available continents
some darker sequence of a world
whose chemical conditions
stand for things

worse than night extended
intending to be mystified
if safer than ground
pulled out from under

tending of minor objects
which shun the light of day
from the world into which we go
otherwise than we thought

or starting with an event
change of air or blue
again removed to make a case

from doubt for the time being
to think what's coming
even while

procedures for relief jammed
into volume craving
to begin with a life's work

before completion
of what might have seemed promiscuous
in a transfer of attributes

to the blue horizon if ever
it happens twice as set
in relief by the living

doing over
what loosely based on life
again resolves

begin with influencing the body

in its nightly advance
under skies of more and more

warmth with face and mouth
we were dreamed in that blue water

available and availing
itself: come again?

out of sight of land to what will
or will not live on

in face of rereading
the waters: to the body: what it wants

to inhabit traces (so you don't
remember) the confusion

we who advanced from private hands
to plea of secrets

Eccentricity of the Middle Ground

covering a given distance, a countryside, is an open conveyance to the
starting point, through the city's edge

to astronomical indices with a memory only for moods, curved, carving

> boundless surface
> zero volume

a character with the gift of disappearance begins a journey on the
available road, occasional slopes and curves, sonic tones in forest
tones, trees breeding branches

> a mark was not upon the air
> coruscating anonym

cartographic graze of continent swimming in horizon line, a populace
flees downhill trailing lives negotiate views, rivulets amid skylines

> one voice sub-vocalizing stood for
the absolute value of singing

> time warms
> accumulating
> midday
> warms light
> stands still sonic
> word blind

infancy held at edge of many stories oversight of fruitful coalition,
perception nestled in coverts misplaces meaning shaken from tectrices

> when wing hits air

feeling as
from a former time, to calculate the distance conveyed above the
surface, beyond gravity's reach, the distance covered and the distance
sustaining apparent reality as in a foreign country

one stops for the night
                    situated at a coast, assembled
characters brush together in notions of rationality foreign to a place;
alarm incites a moment requiring gravity: make travel arrangements
from the sea

                              sub-vocalizing
                              circular research
                              obedient vacillation's
                              tailspin
                              parallel to life

                                        "these people"
were all that remains of shelter leave a wake as in water

                              if only a strange sound
                              would come along
                              the path of fortuity:
                              substitute, prevaricate, suffice

as thought disappears within itself, sequence covers itself, as layers of
the water clear, flinch, shiver

predicate seizure scaling the form, geological final aspect

                    on that flight
                    door opened
                    in came a crowd

                                        invents repose
advancing into the picture plane intimacy of lesser velocity, ocean
slowed to a standstill

                    call, summon, shout
                    ten stories down
                    catenary curve

falls as one for awhile
before dismantling
a species of disarray

modes of transport,

                                                    at first a
scene wanted something: early summer evening or a character with the
gift of anonymity makes a time from the past sound promising: face
value — shuttered light, facades, vacant square, the ocean itself, peaks
shift, lit

                                                            cursive
as a ratio, nest of exchange, breeding transfer

                    what was seen then
                    was never seen again
                    to annul or revive
                    a presiding aura

                            a treeline bows from across a field:
beyond eddies of leaves graze attend reach in

a destination
                            alarm spread assimilation
of laws, of news; from midnight to midnight invasion stands by the sea.
Bring self-possession landward. A first hint of a time out of the past:
will it be more, will it be warm, has it been?

pursues too closely arbitrarily fast transformation, uses, misuses,
overuses a foreign body

                            now please see the sea as it's
left in the past, a road developing a name, the Via Anon, a lapse rate
gradient from the bliss of incomprehension

in long sentences
from another century the characters trail; sensation of easy travel, loss
of a "whole world," a change of scene. Refugees through vacated
outlying areas, some trees, a sequence overlaps, preset as if in antiquity,
a feeling abridged

> branches abroad
> a memory only
> for moods
> fail to recognize
> a difference
> nothing also
> has a face

the front in its infancy, at the window, in the air, in the light, as
gestures' emotional refrain, synalepha

a road renamed all it traveled through; from an elevated passage,
houses amid trees left standing; a dwelling with walls stripped away,
artifacts of possession arranged to express the personality of departure

traveling en masse
is vivacious, off the road, wandering in dust; yellow leaves light
anfractuous landscape, fractious character
populace diffused across a continent, rivers,
rivulets, aerial views delve to the center, time in which to complete the
story runs to ground in the foreground; illustrated artifact

sees the whole curve blue, land
masses swimming, dwelling equal to travelers, marks upon the path
from a cardinally neutral point a destination is conveyed, characters
curve from the map; a list of substances carved from another century,
enigmatic categories, bliss and others

> its circular research
> landward, seaward,
> routines of darkness,

                                    light, fly between latitudes
                                          incite signing
                              of treaties

                                                           in an agitated
state, a thousand miles away obscured from view the sea

                                                           gives way
to a schedule of minor torment, an air of refrain, a refrain of covert
rebellious impulses; within the house characters accumulate
atmosphere of denouement

                                          distance transposed
                                          imaginary synonyms

                                          scrutiny
                                          of lost thought

                                          rotation without a sphere
                                          world blind

                        emotional heterosphere marks instability mixing
suppressed rules of the given from rules of invention, transfer of
momentum through much deeper layers
                                    of to
                                          place characters with the
gift of unanimity breaking forth as a flood to a foreign border amid
city streets; a clandestine crossing

of early summer evening through streets from a former time or a less
elaborate place

                                          lost in a center
                                          begin at the ends

a dry river bed
is the Via Unanima, yellow walls smeared with dust, gallery of sandy
windows

peering through instruments' slow
transpositions modeled on an imagined present, public spaces assigned
to depletion, structures stripped of facades took positions noiselessly

measures
never where it is but where it was
"misgivings fall to the purpose"

by these tactics,
see them less completely predicated, diagrammatic orders of moods
intersecting in the wake of emotional reverses

water spilt glass
smoothes light on
stochastic surface

the one part repels the others eastward, westward,
southward, northward, inward

sees through this thought: a crisis
washed away in its residential aura

when sounds
exchange
conjecture
it's a cloudy science
unanimity resists
resistance

forms possession analogy — form from consonance sound branches —
few form recognizable — most from inherited primitive lost types — of
all or most but went on in the road renamed but lost, wanders as in a
separate language, no conveyances in the streets, route learns itself

through erratic breaches to a crossover point, a changing room, where
characters mass and tend, tend to move in the direction in which they
are embedded through structures as old as natural features

behaving as though
concentrated at one point foreign to a place, trees find eccentric
positions, middle of the road proliferation of disorder, public squares
misguide relation to branch routes inversely proportional to spare the
distance between them

a body of water concealed: rectangular but limitless, surface tamed
except by the sky, reflecting pools, immerses its uses
known to the populace unknown to authorities,
given over to
index of possession proprietary of the broadest sense, anywhere, along
its lateral extent it meets
a purpose beginning to develop contradicts
inadmissible returns
a dialect fractured

until in places a wall was leaving, driving sea strewn for miles

the Via Anomie ends in a glassy surface, swimmers' shining bodies

eustatic reflection
purpose falls to misgivings

circulation's world-
wide morning to
morning pacing
faraway seeks
an ampler space
a light touch
letters put to flight
to sing
the sea quietly withdraws
a crowd

distance exceeding any
ordinary tempo slows

lazy, nearly, water falls from glass, arena falls from sand

falls as a gift with the character of any dimension

this way to a sea, this sea away
guiding through hills of grass
taciturn windward refrain

"and the wind carries it" by analogy or guess no matter how
farfetched: stones at the bottom of the sea were heated by the moon

in gratitude, variously, for
legacies, inspiration, guidance, help of all kinds

Anne Casalino, Annie-Will Siler, Ariana Smart, Barbara Sloan, Beula Bidwell Sloan, Edith Freeman, Frankie Chamberlain, Friederike Retzer, George Sloan, Janice Hirota, Jeb Sloan, Jeff Royer, Jess, Jorge Esquinca, Kathleen Fraser, Larry Casalino, Marcy Alancraig, Marie LaManna Plimpton, Mary Plimpton Sloan, Michael Palmer, Nina Hemenway, Norma Cole, Penny Downes, Pete Adelman, Rick London, Robert Duncan, Sam Earnshaw, Susan Gevirtz, Susan Griffin, Susan Howe, Susan Richardson, Todd Baron, Tom Mandel

Other Chax Books

Myung Mi Kim, *The Bounty*
Kathleen Fraser, *When New Time Folds Up*
Norman Fischer, *Precisely the Point Being Made*
Nathaniel Tarn, *Caja del Rio*
Rosmarie Waldrop, *Fan Poem for Deshika*
Lisa Cooper, *The Ballad in Memory*
Nathaniel Mackey, *Outlantish*
Ron Silliman, *Demo to Ink*
Beverly Dahlen, *A Reading 8 – 10*
Gil Ott, *Wheel*
Karen Mac Cormack, *Quirks & Quillets*
Susan Bee & Charles Bernstein, *Fool's Gold*
Sheila Murphy, *Teth*
bp Nichol, *Art Facts: A Book of Contexts*
Charles Bernstein, *Four Poems*
Larry Evers & Felipe S. Molina, *Wo'i Bwikam/Coyote Songs*
Mei-mei Berssenbrugge, *Mizu*
Charles Alexander, *Hopeful Buildings*
Lyn Hejinian & Kit Robinson, *Individuals*
Eli Goldblatt, *Sessions*
John Randolph Hall, *Zootaxy*
Paul Metcalf, *Firebird*
Karl Young, *Five Kwaidan in Sleeve Pages*
Charles Alexander, *Two Songs*
Paul Metcalf, *Golden Delicious*
Jackson Mac Low, *French Sonnets*

Forthcoming in 1995 & 1996 —

Hank Lazer, *Three of Ten*
Karen Mac Cormack, *Marine Snow*
Lisa Cooper, *& Calling It Snow*